Afrocentric Self Inventory and Discovery Workbook for African American Youth

AFROCENTRIC SELF INVENTORY AND DISCOVERY WORKBOOK FOR AFRICAN AMERICAN YOUTH (AGES 12 - 15)

DEVELOPED BY
USENI EUGENE PERKINS

First Edition
Second Printing

Cover design by Cheryl Y. Catlin

Cover photography by James Ray

Dedicated to All Youth of African Descent

Acknowledgement

Special thanks to Brenda Polk for typing manuscript

Third World Press
7524 South Cottage Grove Avenue
Chicago, IL 60619

OTHER BOOKS BY USENI EUGENE PERKINS

- Home Is A Dirty Street: The Social Oppression of Black Children (1976)

- Harvesting New Generations: The Positive Development of Black Youth (1988)

- Explosion of Chicago's Black Street Gangs (1988)

- Afrocentric Self Inventory and Discovery Workbook for African American Youth (1989)

- Explosion In The Streets: A Manual On Black Street Gangs (1989)

- When You Grow Up: Poems For Black Children (1984)

- We Have Been There Before: A Poetic Narrative Through Black History

TABLE OF CONTENTS

INTRODUCTION

This workbook is for you -- the African American youth -- to help you better understand and appreciate yourself, our people and your place in the universe. It is intended to help you become a stronger, more intelligent and better person so you can achieve your true potential and be an asset to your community. This workbook is designed to do two things. First, it will help you to make an inventory of yourself as it relates to certain principles that are considered to be desirable for African American youth. Secondly, it will help you to discover new things that should help you to better appreciate your beautiful culture and heritage.

I hope that as you use this manual you will examine it very closely, study hard and try to apply some of its principles to yourself.

You are a very special person who represents the future for all people of African descent. Therefore, it's important that you prepare yourself today so you can best meet the challenges you will face tomorrow.

In the interest and welfare
of African American youth,

Useni Eugene Perkins

YOUTH

We have tomorrow
Bright before us
Like a flame.

Yesterday
A night-gone thing
A sun-down name.

And dawn-today
Broad arch above the road we came.

We march!

Langston Hughes

I. MEANING OF AFROCENTRICITY

Afrocentricity is about the social, historical, cultural and spiritual development of people of African descent. It is a way of looking at yourself differently from the way other people may see you. Indeed, Afrocentricity helps you to better understand and appreciate who you are and how you can improve yourself.

Afrocentricity is both old and new. That is to say, it celebrates our beautiful heritage and praises the best of our culture which we have today.

The development of Afrocentricity can be contributed to many brothers and sisters, some of whom are:

- Dr. Maulana Karenga
- Dr. Molefi Kete Asante
- Dr. Vivian Gordon
- Haki Madhubuti
- Dr. Wade Nobles
- Dr. Robert L. Williams
- Dr. Nsenga Warfield-Coppack
- Mafari Moore
- Gwen Akua Gilyard
- Dr. Morris X Jeff
- Dr. Aminifu Harvey
- Hannibal Tirus Afrik
- Abena Joan Brown
- Kamau Anderson
- Dr. Margaret Burroughs

Of course there are many other brothers and sisters who have contributed to the development of Afrocentricity. This is important to understand because it shows that it is collective in its origin.

So that you will have a better understanding of Afrocentricity, the following terms are being provided:

- KEMET — The original name of Egypt where people of African descent created the world's first great civilizations.

- **NUBIA** — An ancient name used to identify the continent we now call Africa.

- **AFRICA** — The common name now used to identify the continent where people of African descent originated.

- **AFRICAN** — A person of African descent who is a citizen of one of the countries in Africa. Examples: Nigerian, Ghanaian, Ethiopian, Senegalese.

- **TRIBE** — A sub-group of an African country that speaks its own language. For example, in Nigeria there are the Hausa, Fulani, Igbo and Yoruba tribes.

- **AFRICAN AMERICAN** — A person of color who is a citizen of America and whose ancestors originated on the continent of Africa.

- **DIASPORA** — The dispersement of people of African descent throughout the world.

- **NGUZO SABA** — A Black value system created by Dr. Maulana Karenga.

- **MOTHERLAND** — The continent of Africa and homeland for people of African descent.

- **ANCESTORS** — Those who have died and whose spirits continue to provide us understanding and direction.

- **ETHOS** — Our collective self-consciousness and collective personality that celebrates our national origin as a people.

- **MYTHOLOGY** — Stories and legends about our ancestors, heroes and heroines who have contributed to our greatness as a people.

- COSMOLOGY	The foundation for our thinking, beliefs, perceptions and values.
- WEUSI	The collective Black mind as defined by Dr. Robert Williams.
- ELDER	An older adult who gives wisdom and guidance to youth.
- ONTOLOGY	Emphasizes our collective identity, collective struggle and collective destiny.
- RITES OF PASSAGE	A formal process for educating and grooming young boys and girls for adulthood.
- PROVERBS	Oral wisdom passed down from generation to generation.
- CULTURE	The basis for one's behavior, attitudes and values. Culture helps to define who you are and who you are not.
- LIBERATION	Freedom for all people of African descent.
- STRUGGLE	Commitment to work in behalf of all people of African descent.
- LIBATION	The act of pouring a liquid on the soil to give respect to and praise our ancestors.
- PAN-AFRICAN	A person of African descent who believes there is a cultural bond and common struggle that is shared by all African people.
- EUROCENTRIC	A view of the world that expresses the culture, values, history and interest of Europeans.

II. BLACK VALUE SYSTEM (NGUZO SABA) -- CREATED BY DR. MAULANA KARENGA, SEPTEMBER 7, 1965

What is a Value System? -- A value system is a set of principles that guides a person in his and her day-to-day life experiences. It helps you to determine what you should do and what you should not do. When one has a positive value system, he or she is more likely to do positive things. This is the reason we like for you to become familiar with the Nguzo Saba.

The Afrocentric Value System is based on the Nguzo Saba because it helps people of African American descent to work together, respect each other and promote and celebrate our collective history, identity and struggle.

The seven principles of the Nguzo Saba are:

1. Umoja (Unity) -- To strive for and maintain unity in the family, community, nation and race.

2. Kujichagulia (Self-Determination) -- To define ourselves, name ourselves, create for ourselves and speak for ourselves instead of being defined, named, created for and spoken for by others.

3. Ujima (Collective Work and Responsibility) -- To build and maintain our community together and make our sister's and brother's problems our problems and to solve them together.

4. Ujamma (Cooperative Economics) -- To build and maintain our own stores, shops and other businesses and profit from them together.

5. Nia (Purpose) -- To make our collective vocation the building and developing of our community in order to restore our people to their traditional greatness.

6. Kuumba (Creativity) -- To do always as much as we can, in the way we can, in order to leave our community more beautiful and beneficial than we inherited it.

7. Imani (Faith) -- To believe with all our heart in our people, our parents, our teachers, our leaders and the righteousness and victory of our struggle.

Describe below how you might include each principle of the Nguzo Saba in your daily experiences.

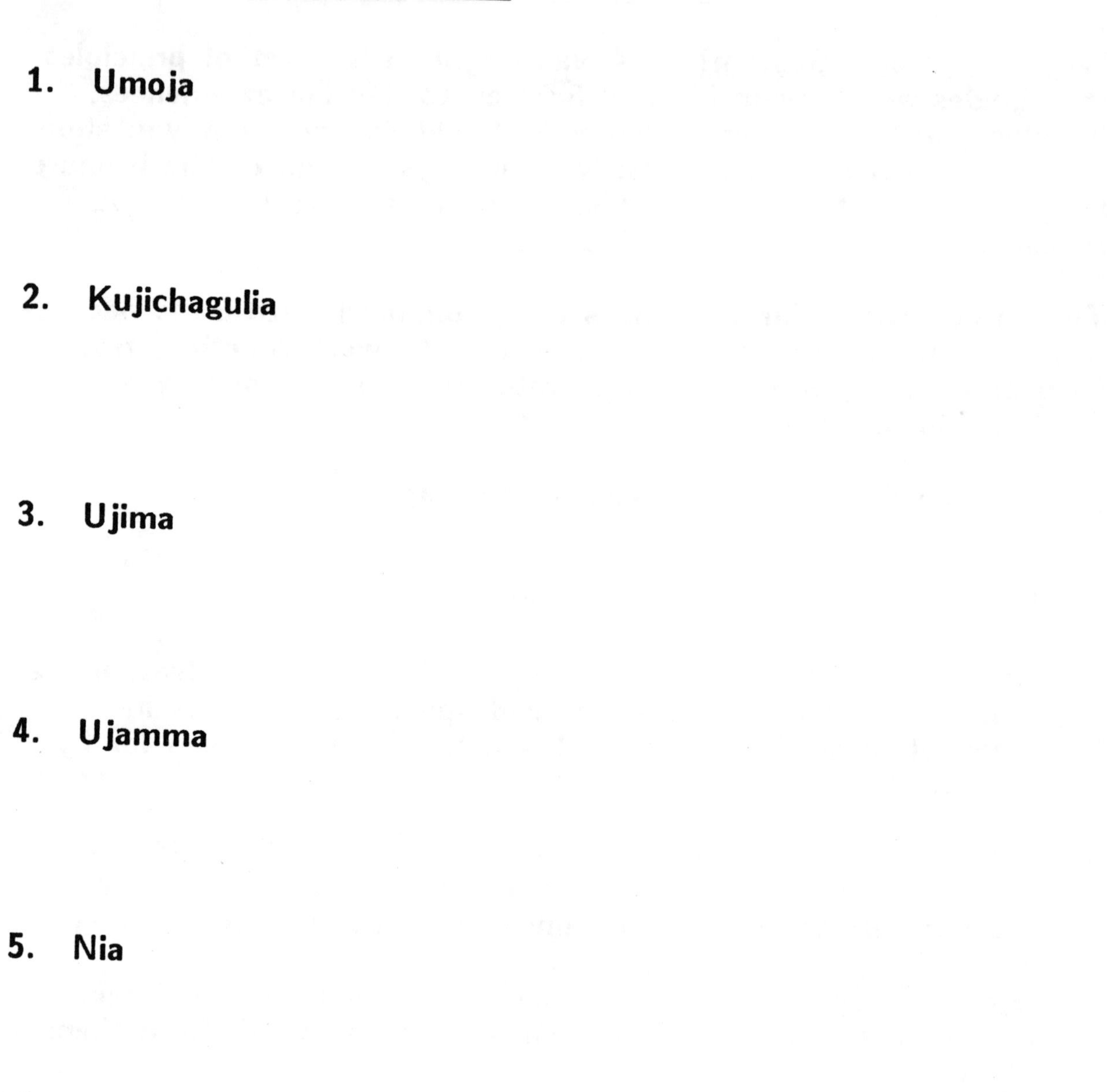

1. **Umoja**

2. **Kujichagulia**

3. **Ujima**

4. **Ujamma**

5. **Nia**

6. **Kuumba**

7. **Imani**

III. AFROCENTRIC SELF-ESTEEM

What is Self-Esteem?

Self-esteem helps to tell you how you feel about yourself. People with low self-esteem normally do not feel too good about themselves. People who have high self-esteem generally feel real good about themselves.

A self-esteem that is guided by Afrocentric principles will help you to:

1. Be proud of whom you are.

2. Feel positive about yourself.

3. Never feel inferior to anyone.

4. Do well in school.

5. Have respect for yourself.

6. Respect your parents and elders.

To help you judge your Afrocentric self-esteem, please answer the following questions:

1. People of African descent are a minority in the world.

   Yes_____ No_____

2. People of African descent built the world's first great civilizations.

   Yes_____ No_____

3. I believe I'm a very special person.

   Yes_____ No_____

4. I'm as good if not better than people of other races.

   Yes_____ No_____

5. I can be a good student if I want to be.

   Yes_____ No_____

6. I like my skin color the way it is.

   Yes_____ No_____

7. I have pride in my race.

   Yes_____ No_____

8. I believe I can accept difficult challenges.

   Yes_____ No_____

9. I have pride in myself.

   Yes_____ No_____

10. I can feel good about myself without using alcohol or drugs.

    Yes_____ No_____

See Page 49 for the appropriate answers to these questions.

IV. KNOWING YOUR FAMILY TREE

Since the publication of Alex Haley's best-selling book, Roots in 1976, there has been an increased interest among African Americans to trace their family heritage. In Roots, Alex Haley traced his family heritage over seven generations to a small village named Juffure in Gambia, West Africa. While few people will be able to achieve what Mr. Haley did, it is possible for many of us to trace our family tree over two or three generations. In traditional African societies, the family tree is also known as the extended family because it includes all those persons who have some direct blood relationship with your family. Doing a family tree can be both educational and fun. To help you trace your family tree, become acquainted with the following terms.

- GENEALOGY — The science of documenting one's family ancestry.
- ANCESTRY — Members of your family tree that helped to shape your heritage.
- GENERATION — The average span of time between the birth of parents and their children.
- MATRIARCH — The family tree on your mother's side.
- PATRIARCH — The family tree on your father's side.
- SIBLING — Your brother and sister.
- MATERNAL AUNT OR UNCLE — Related to your mother.
- PATERNAL AUNT OR UNCLE — Related to your father.
- COUSINS — Children of your aunts and uncles.

There are several ways to begin tracing your family tree, some of which are listed below:

1. If either of your grandparents are living, ask them to tell you about their parents.
2. If your grandparents are not living, ask your parents to tell you about them.
3. If you are living with an aunt or uncle, ask them to tell you about your parents.

Now that you have gotten this basic information, fill in the spaces of the following charts. Remember one chart is for your mother's side and the other is for your father's side.

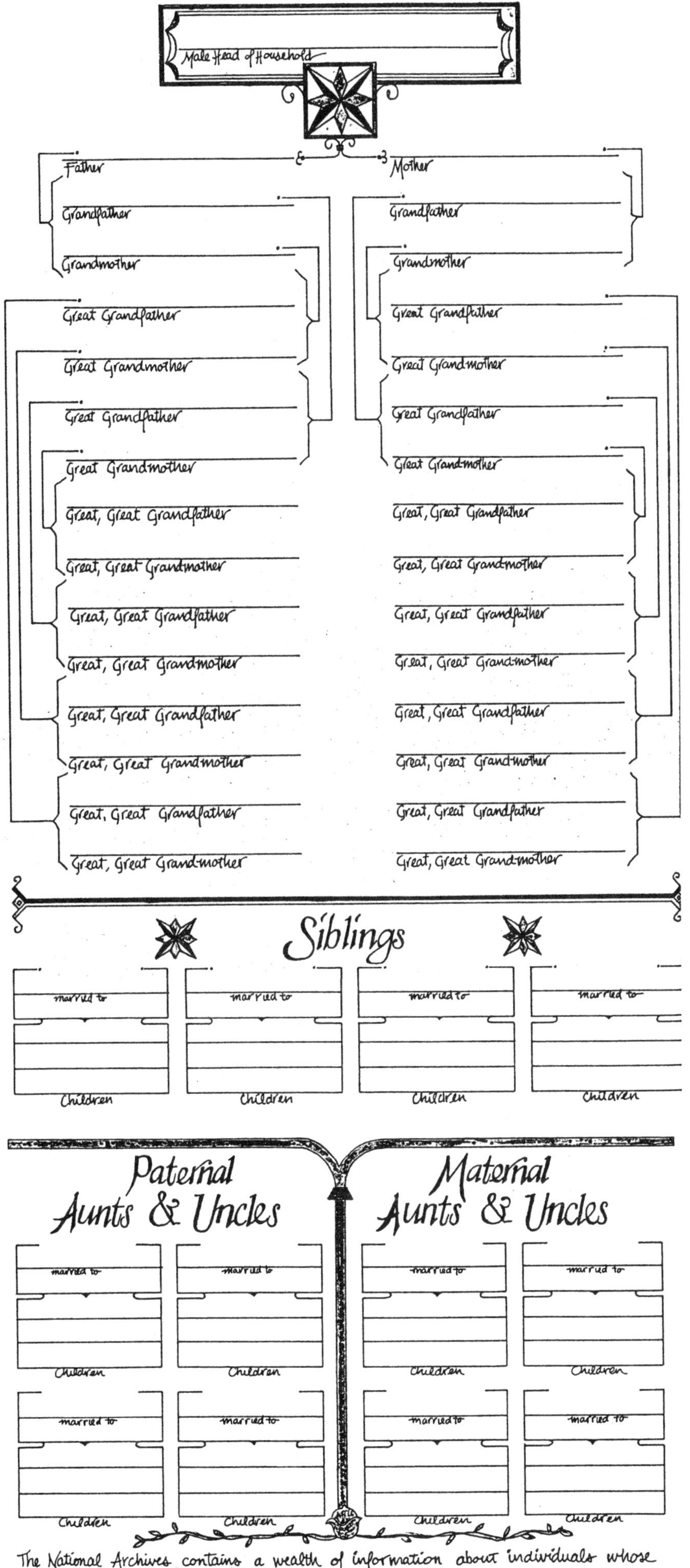

Male Head of Household

Father

Grandfather

Grandmother

Great Grandfather

Great Grandmother

Great Grandfather

Great Grandmother

Great, Great Grandfather

Great, Great Grandmother

Great, Great Grandfather

Great, Great Grandmother

Great, Great Grandfather

Great, Great Grandmother

Great, Great Grandfather

Great, Great Grand-mother

Mother

Grandfather

Grandmother

Great Grandfather

Great Grandmother

Great Grandfather

Great Grandmother

Great, Great Grandfather

Great, Great Grandmother

Great, Great Grandfather

Great, Great Grand-mother

Great, Great Grandfather

Great, Great Grandmother

Great, Great Grandfather

Great, Great Grand-mother

Siblings

married to

Children

married to

Children

married to

Children

married to

Children

Paternal Aunts & Uncles

married to

Children

married to

Children

married to

Children

married to

Children

Maternal Aunts & Uncles

married to

Children

married to

Children

married to

Children

married to

Children

The National Archives contains a wealth of information about individuals whose names appear in Federal records.

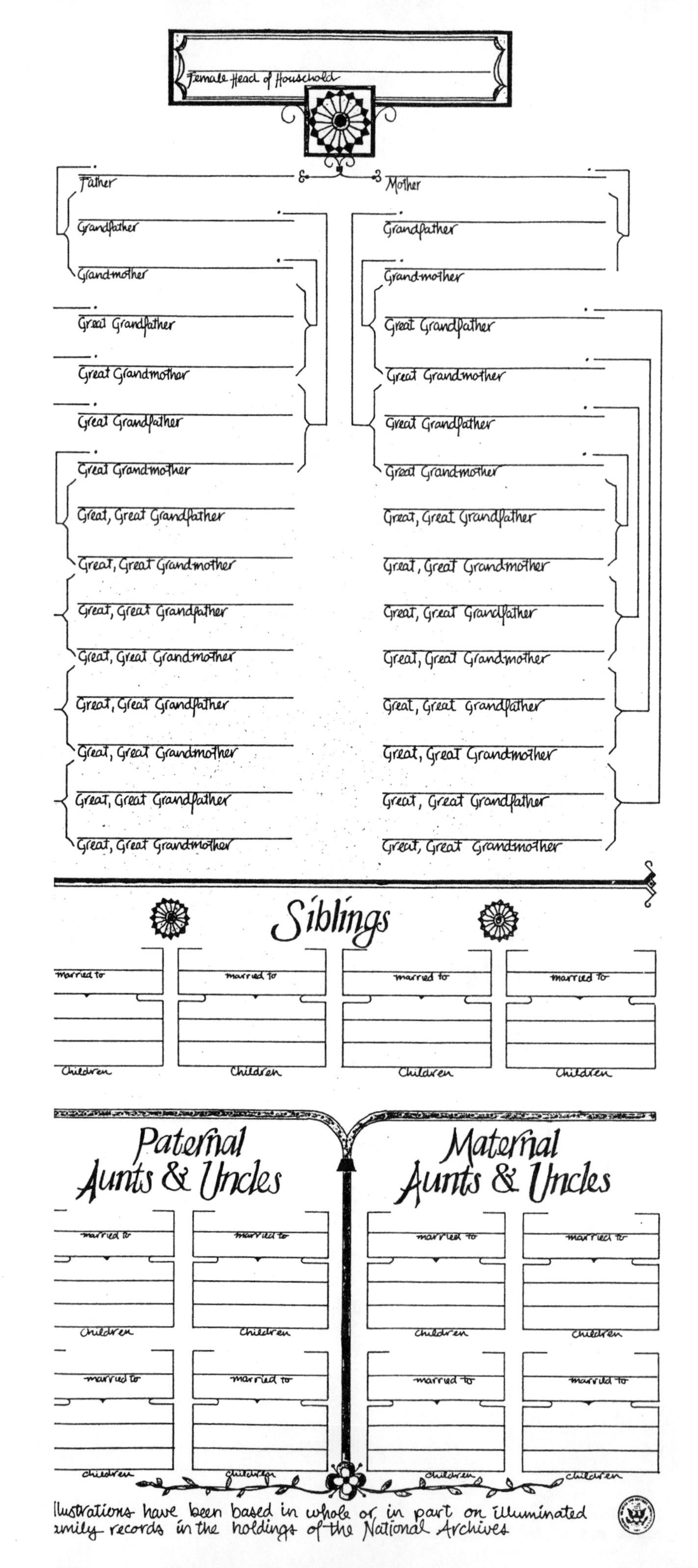
Female Head of Household
Father
Mother
Grandfather
Grandmother
Grandfather
Grandmother
Great Grandfather
Great Grandmother
Great Grandfather
Great Grandmother
Great Grandfather
Great Grandmother
Great Grandfather
Great Grandmother
Great, Great Grandfather
Great, Great Grandmother
Great, Great Grandfather
Great, Great Grandmother
Great, Great Grandfather
Great, Great Grandmother
Great, Great Grandfather
Great, Great Grandmother
Great, Great Grandfather
Great, Great Grandmother
Great, Great Grandfather
Great, Great Grandmother
Great, Great Grandfather
Great, Great Grandmother
Great, Great Grandfather
Great, Great Grandmother
Siblings
married to
Children
Paternal Aunts & Uncles
Maternal Aunts & Uncles
married to
Children
Illustrations have been based in whole or in part on illuminated
family records in the holdings of the National Archives

Do not be discouraged if you are unable to fill all of the spaces. Very few people are able to do that. However, as you become older and develop a greater interest in your family tree, you may also want to check the following documents:

1. Family Bible (before 1900) if you have one.

2. Old letters and diaries.

3. Birth and death certificates.

4. Deeds, wills and other documents.

5. Marriage and divorce records.

6. News clippings about family members.

7. Any letter (before 1900) from or to family members.

8. Church and cemetery records.

Finally, you can visit the United States Department of Archives in Washington, D.C. to obtain additional information.

Do the best you can, and have fun while you are doing it.

V. AFROCENTRIC DEVELOPMENTAL ACTIVITIES

As a young person, you are undergoing an important stage in your social development. It is a stage that begins to prepare you for adulthood. During this period, there are some activities that will help you become a strong and beautiful adult. Some of these activities are listed below with a brief description of each. Whenever possible, try to participate in these activities. If they are not available to you, ask your church, school, social service center or family to organize them for you and your friends.

Manhood and Womanhood Training

A person does not become a man or a woman simply because of his or her chronological and physiological development. Becoming a man or woman is an educational process that can best be learned by emulating men and women who have (respect for themselves) become positive role models for African American youth. As you grow older, follow your parents' example and the example of other positive men and women in your community. For young males, this is especially important because too many associate manhood with being macho and taking advantage of others. In traditional African societies, the community assumed a shared responsibility for helping youth become men and women. This is often done through a "rites of passage" program that prepares youth for adulthood. Consult your church or community agency to develop a rites of passage program. For additional information on rites of passage see the list of reference books on Page 51.

Spiritual Enrichment

People of African descent are very spiritual. We generally have deep feelings about religion and our relationship with the universe. Our spirituality dates back to ancient Kemet (Egypt) when we worshipped nature's beauty and paid homage to our Creator. Being a spiritual people has also made us strong so we can endure many hardships and continue to survive. As spiritual people, it's important that we express our true feelings. We want you to be able to express your true feelings, too. It will make you a much stronger person and help you to have compassion for life. Regardless of how difficult things may be, our spirituality will help us to "weather the storm" and be in touch with our Creator.

Cultural Enrichment

Haki Madhubuti, an internationally acclaimed poet and publisher of Third World Press, has said, "The best way to fight an alien culture, is to live your own." This simply means that having a knowledge and appreciation of your own culture will better help you to be your natural self. By being your natural self you will be closer linked to your true culture and heritage. Cultural enrichment is more than just knowing about popular culture and listening to the latest records, watching T.V. and going to the movies. It is having a knowledge of your heritage and understanding how it can help you appreciate the greatness of African American people. For more information on African American culture, turn to Page 31.

Educational Reinforcement

To help you perform better in school, you may need to get assistance. Sometimes assistance can come from your parents, brothers and sisters or a tutor. In some Black communities, there are independent Black schools which can assist you in your educational development. In fact, even if you are doing well in school, you can benefit from these Black institutions because they also teach you to have a better understanding and appreciation of your heritage and culture. This should be important to you because often the public schools do not teach these things. Of course you can also do some independent reading to increase your knowledge. On Page 51 we have listed a few books which should be of interest to you.

Education remains one of the important cornerstones for achieving success. Get as much education and knowledge as you can. As you become older, you'll never regret it.

Financial Management

Money is not necessarily "the root of all evil." If you use it properly, it can help you do a lot of things. African Americans spend nearly 30 billion dollars a year. However, we do not produce many products or manufacture items that will enable us to have successful businesses. However, if you begin now to properly manage the little money you have, when you become older you could own your own business. I realize it's not easy to save money --

but if you could open a savings account you will never regret it. If African Americans are going to be active participants in the economy, we must begin to make better use of the money we do earn.

Sex Education

Sex plays a very important role in our lives. When we understand its true function and use it properly, it can help us to become beautiful people. However, when we do not understand its true function and use it improperly it can create problems that we are unprepared to meet. First, you must learn to appreciate sex as a part of your physical development and not just as a means to have a sexual relationship with the opposite sex. Sex is also respecting your body as well as the body of others. It has been given to us by the Creator so each of us can be a fully developed human being and not as a means to exploit and abuse others. As a young person, you are going through a very critical period in your sexual development. Try to understand and control your sexual emotions so that you will not regret something you may do today at a later date. Also, remember that your health is extremely important and one must be extremely careful in relating to other people. If you can, enroll in a sex education class.

Racial Awareness

Knowing who you are is extremely important. It helps you to appreciate your heritage and culture and to have respect for other members of your race. People of African descent live throughout the world and having an awareness of your racial origin will help you to relate to them. For example, most likely you have seen or met a few Africans. If so, did you extend a welcome to them and accept them as your brothers and sisters? The same type of greeting should be extended to brothers and sisters who live in the West Indies or other parts of the world. As people of Africa descent, we all have something in common. Also, having an appreciation of your race will help you to do things that best serve the interest of our people. Until all people of African descent are free, none of us are free.

Physical Fitness Training

For you to become a strong and beautiful person, you must be physically fit. Your body is like a car -- it needs to be cared for if it is to properly function. To keep yourself in good physical shape, enroll in a physical fitness program, eat nourishing food, do not drink, smoke, or use drugs and get proper rest. Following are a few things you can do to keep in good shape:

- Exercise daily so you can do at least 10 push-ups.

- Exercise so you can run at least two miles.

- Participate on an athletic team.

- Have a physical check-up each year.

Health Maintenance

It has been said that what you are is largely due to what you eat. Eating the correct food is important to helping you be a strong, healthy and beautiful person. Health maintenance is related to physical fitness because it, too, emphasizes the importance of keeping your body in good shape. But good health maintenance also takes into consideration your emotional being and helps to reduce the stress in your life. Because of the racism faced by African Americans, many have high blood pressure which may lead to other serious health problems. In fact, the average life span of African Americans is 2 - 8 years shorter than it is for whites. As the future leaders of the African American community, we need you to be as healthy as you possibly can to ensure we will survive as a people.

VI. SPECIAL DAYS TO CELEBRATE

Throughout the year, there are special days that people of African descent should celebrate. These days give us an opportunity to pay tribute to special people and events which have contributed to our struggle. Listed below are a few of these special days. A brief description is given so you can plan a special activity for each. If you are not familiar with some of these people or events -- then do some research on them so you will understand why they are important.

January

01 Founding of the African Benevolent Society - 1808.

15 Dr. Martin Luther King Jr.'s Birthday - 1929.

February

14 Freedom Fighter Frederick Douglass born - 1817.

19 First Pan-African Congress organized in Paris by W.E.B. DuBois - 1919.

March

03 Richard Allen founded the African Methodist and Episcopal Church - 1794.

12 Jean Baptiste Pointe De Sable, first non-Indian to settle in Chicago - 1773.

April

09 Paul Robeson, activist, singer, scholar and freedom fighter, born - 1898.

29 Duke Ellington, famous musician and composer, born - 1899.

May

02 Elijah McCoy, inventor who held over 50 patents, born - 1844.

19 Malcolm X, political activist, born - 1925.

June

16 Denmark Vesey led slave rebellion in Charleston, South Carolina - 1822.

27 Paul Laurence Dunbar, poet and novelist, born - 1872.

July

11 Niagra Movement founded - 1905.

28 Fourteenth Amendment was adopted, making Blacks American citizens - 1868.

August

17 Marcus Garvey, Pan-Africanist freedom fighter and founder of Universal Nationalist Improvement Association, born - 1887.

21 Nat Turner, freedom fighter, led rebellion in Southampton, Virginia - 1831.

September

15 First National Negro Convention began in Philadelphia - 1830.

18 Congress passed Fugitive Slave Act as part of the Compromise - 1850.

October

02 Robert H. Lawrence, first African American astronaut, born - 1935.

06 Fannie Lou Hamer, freedom fighter, born - 1917.

November

05 Negro History Week was initiated by Carter G. Woodson - 1926.

05 Shirley Chisholm became first African American woman elected to Congress - 1968.

December

01 Montgomery Bus Boycott begun by Rosa Parks - 1955.

12 "Lift Every Voice and Sing" composed by James Weldon Johnson - 1900.

VII. AFROCENTRIC COMMUNITY SERVICE PROJECTS

One of the most important features of Afrocentricity is that it is collective in its thought, actions and purpose. This simply means we must also help others in our community as we help ourselves. Community service helps you to fulfill this principle and express the value of KUUMBA. On the following pages, you will have an opportunity to develop several community service projects. Get the assistance of your friends whenever you can. Try and do at least one community service project each month. Some suggestions for community service projects are:

1. Do errands for the elderly.
2. Help clean up your neighborhood.
3. Volunteer to help a sick person.
4. Tutor a younger student.
5. Volunteer to help your church, school or social agency.

Describe your Monthly Community Service Project:

January

Type of Project:

Activity Performed:

February

Type of Project:

Activity Performed:

March

Type of Project:

Activity Performed:

April

Type of Project:

Activity Performed:

May

Type of Project:

Activity Performed:

June

Type of Project:

Activity Performed:

July

Type of Project:

Activity Performed:

August

Type of Project:

Activity Performed:

September

Type of Project:

Activity Performed:

October

Type of Project:

Activity Performed:

November

Type of Project:

Activity Performed:

December

Type of Project:

Activity Performed:

VIII. AFROCENTRIC EXERCISES

Identity

The identity of a person is very important. It helps you to know who you are and who you are not. It also helps you to acknowledge your heritage and your culture. As a person of African descent, you have been given many identities, some of which are:

1. Slave
2. Colored
3. Negro
4. Afro-American
5. Black
6. African American
7. African

Which one of the above best describes who you are?

Why did you make this choice?

Name three people in your life that have had the greatest influence on you.

Name three African Americans whom you admire and explain why.

1.

2.

3.

What do you like most about being a person of African descent?

What would you like to be when you become an adult? Why?

What do you know about the Civil Rights Movement? Explain.

What do you know about the Black Power Movement? Explain.

Name three things you like to do most.

1.

2.

3.

What are your three favorite subjects?

1.

2.

3.

Name three African countries.

1.

2.

3.

Name three of your favorite books.

1.

2.

3.

Name three of your favorite television shows.

1.

2.

3.

Name three things that make you feel good.

1.

2.

3.

Name three things that make you feel bad.

1.

2.

3.

IX. APPRECIATION OF AFRICAN AMERICAN CULTURE

The culture of African Americans has a rich legacy, heritage and tradition. Its roots can be traced to the oldest organized cultures in the history of mankind. It is a culture that has contributed outstanding art, literature, poetry, music, architecture, and dance to the world. It is a culture that shines with creativity and celebrates, entertains and educates so we can always be a proud and beautiful people.

To help you better understand and appreciate African American culture, some examples are being provided for you.

THE NEGRO SPEAKS OF RIVERS

I've known rivers:
I've known rivers ancient as the world and older than
    the flow of human blood in human veins.

My soul has grown deep like the rivers.

I bathed in the Euphrates when dawns were young.
I built my hut near the Congo and it lulled me to sleep.
I looked upon the Nile and raised the pyramids above it.
I heard the singing of the Mississippi when Abe Lincoln
    went down to New Orleans, and I've seen its
    muddy bosom turn all golden in the sunset.

I've known rivers:
Ancient, dusky rivers.

    My soul has grown deep like the rivers.

Langston Hughes

RESPONSE TO POEM

1. Did you like the poem? Yes_____ No_____

   Why?

2. On what continent is the Nile River?

3. Who built the first pyramids?

4. What is meant by "when dawns were young?"

* LIFT EVERY VOICE AND SING

Lift every voice and sing
Till earth and heaven ring,
Ring with the harmonies of Liberty;
Let our rejoicing rise
High as the listening skies,
Let it resound loud as the rolling sea.
Sing a song full of the faith that the dark past has taught us,
Sing a song full of the hope that the present has brought us,
Facing the rising sun of our new day begun
Let us march on till victory is won.

Stony the road we trod,
Bitter the chastening rod,
Felt in the days when hope unborn had died;
Yet with a steady beat,
Have not our weary feet
Come to the place for which our fathers sighed?
We have come over a way that with tears has been watered,
We have come, treading our path through the blood of the slaughtered,
Out from the gloomy past,
Till now we stand at last
Where the white gleam of our bright star is cast.

God of our weary years,
God of our silent tears,
Thou who hast brought us thus far on the way;
Thou who hast by Thy might
Led us into the light,
Keep us forever in the path, we pray.
Lest our feet stray from the places, our God, where we met Thee,
Lest, our hearts drunk with the wine of the world, we forget Thee;
Shadowed beneath Thy hand,
May we forever stand.
True to our God,
True to our native land.

James Weldon Johnson

* This poem has been put to music
and is now our Black National Anthem.

RESPONSE TO POEM

1. **Did you like the poem? Yes_____ No_____**

   Why?

2. **What is meant by "stony the road we trod?"**

3. **What is meant by "the blood of the slaughtered?"**

MOTHER TO SON

Well, son, I'll tell you:
Life for me ain't been no crystal stair.
It's had tacks in it,
And splinters,
And boards torn up,
And places with no carpet on the floor --
Bare.
But all the time
I'se been a-climbin' on,
And reachin' landin's,
and turnin' corners,
And sometimes goin' in the dark
Where there ain't been no light.
So, boy, don't you turn back.
Don't you set down on the steps
'Cause you finds it kinder hard.
Don't you fall now --
For I'se still goin', honey,
I'se still climbin',
And life for me ain't been no crystal stair.

Langston Hughes

RESPONSE TO POEM

1. Did you like the poem? Yes_____ No_____

   Why?

2. What is meant by a "crystal stair?"

3. What message is the mother trying to convey?

WHAT IS AFRICA TO ME

What is Africa to me:
Copper sun or scarlet sea,
Jungle star or jungle track,
Strong bronzed men, or regal black
Women from whose loins I sprang
When the birds of Eden sang?
One, three centuries removed
From the scene his father loved,
Spicy grove, cinnamon tree,
What is Africa to me?

Countee Cullen

RESPONSE TO POEM

1. Did you like the poem? Yes_____ No_____

   Why?

2. How does the poem relate to African Americans?

3. What is Africa to you?

FAMOUS QUOTATIONS OF INSPIRATION AND STRUGGLE

It is very important that you have a "sense of struggle" so you can focus your energy in the right direction. At this point in your life, your struggle should be to study hard and develop your mind. By doing this, you will better understand what struggle is actually about, and how you can best participate. Following are several inspirational quotations by courageous African Americans who have contributed to our struggle.

- **"Let me give you a word of the philosophy of reforms. The whole history of the progress of human liberty shows that all concessions, yet made to her august claims, have been born of earnest struggle. If there is no struggle there is no progress."**

  From Frederick Douglass' letter to Gerret Smith, 1849.

- **"Let your motto be resistance! Resistance! Resistance! No oppressed people have ever secured their liberty without resistance."**

  Henry Garnet, Call to Rebellion, 1843.

- **"Fear not the number and education of our enemies, against whom we shall have to contend for our lawful right; guaranteed to us by our Maker; for why should we be afraid, when God is, and will continue (if we continue humble) to be on our side?"**

  From David Walker's Appeal, 1829.

- **"We have reached the time when every minute, every second must count for something done, something achieved in the cause of Africa. We need the freedom of Africa now."**

  Marcus Garvey, Philosophy and Opinions, 1923.

- "We are glad to be Black. We rejoice in the darkness of our skin, we celebrate the natural texture of our hair, we extol the rhythm and vigor of our songs and shouts and dances."

Vincent Harding, 1968.

- "Our fight for peace in America is a fight for human dignity, and an end to ghetto life. It is the fight for the constitutional liberties, the civil and human rights of every American."

Paul Robeson, July 20, 1949.

Write a statement that reflects your commitment to struggle.

AFRICAN AMERICAN SPIRITUALS AND GOSPEL MUSIC

The spirituals and gospel music have both been historically linked with the development of Black music in America. This distinction is indeed correct because both are the creations of Black people and date as far back as the beginning of slavery. However, although the spiritual and gospel began in America, we know for a fact they were greatly influenced by African music. The spiritual and gospel are both joyful and sad music. When the first slaves were brought to America and the West Indies, they sung songs about their miseries and struggles. After being forced to work in cotton fields, they sung songs which gave them strength to overcome the inhumane conditions inflicted upon them by their white slavemasters. While both of these forms of music had a strong religious orientation, they managed to reflect other feelings not normally associated with religion. It has often been said that the spiritual and gospel helped Black people to survive over the past four hundred years. While this may not be entirely true, it is a fact that the spiritual and gospel provided Black people with an inspirational force.

Today, the spiritual and gospel continue to be an inspiration to many Black people. Throughout Black America this vibrant music can be heard, sung and played in Black churches. It is a music that all Black people should appreciate because within the spiritual and gospel contain many of the hardships, joys and sadness that have been a part of the Black man's life in America.

1. Name two spirituals that you know.

   a.

   b.

2. Is there a relationship between spirituals and gospel music and the blues and rhythm and blues? Explain.

3. What types of music do you enjoy? Why?

AFRICAN PROVERBS

It has been said that proverbs are the daughters of experience, which simply means they represent truth and wisdom that reflects real life. We can learn a lot from proverbs for they provide us with values and understanding which can better help us to make wise decisions.

Following are some African proverbs for you to learn. After reading each proverb, write a few lines to explain what it means to you.

Ghana (Ashanti)

"When you follow in the path of your father, you learn to walk like him."

Meaning:

"The ruins of a nation begins in the homes of its people."

Meaning:

Cameroon

"By trying often, the monkey learns to jump from the tree."

Meaning:

"Knowledge is better than riches."

Meaning:

Zaire

"Children are the reward of life."

Meaning:

"The friends of our friends are our friends."

Meaning:

Ethiopia

"One who runs alone cannot be outrun by another."

Meaning:

"Anticipate the good so that you may enjoy it."

Meaning:

Kenya

"Do not say the first thing that comes to your mind."

Meaning

"It is the duty of children to wait on elders, and not the elders wait on children."

Meaning:

Nigeria

"The day on which one starts out is not the time to start one's preparations."

Meaning:

"What the child says, he has heard at home."

Meaning:

TRADITIONAL AFRICAN NAMES

In traditional African societies, the naming of a newborn child was considered to be an important event. Therefore, much time and patience were taken to give a child a name that best describes the child at birth, or represents a special event, day or in honor of a relative. In recent years, many African Americans have adopted African names either at birth or during a period in their lives. For some African Americans this is a way for them to show their relationship with their motherland. However, you do not have to adopt an African name to prove you are of African descent. But for those who choose to do so, a list of African names is being provided:

African Female Names

Name	Pronunciation	Meaning	Language and Country
Abayomi	ah-BAH-yoh-mee	Pleasant meeting	Yoruba, Nigeria
Abena	ah-beh-NAH	Born on Tuesday	Fante, Ghana
Adeleke	ah-DEH-leh-keh	Crown achieves happiness	Yoruba, Nigeria
Akosua	ah-KOH-soo-ah	Born on Sunday	Ewe, Ghana
Ashura	ah-SHOO-rah	Born during Islamic month Ashur	Swahili, E. Africa
Dalila	dah-LEE-lah	Gentle	Swahili, E. Africa
Fatima	FAH-tee-mah	Daughter of the Prophet	Arabic, N. Africa
Foluke	foh-LOO-keh	Placed in God's care	Yoruba, Nigeria

Ife	ee-FEH	Love	Yoruba, Nigeria
Jamila	jah-MEE-lah	Beautiful	Swahili, E. Africa
Karimah	kah-REE-mah	Generous	Arabic, N. Africa
Mandisa	man-DEE-sah	Sweet	Xhosa, S. Africa
Olabisi	oh-LAH-bee-see	Joy is multiplied	Yoruba, Nigeria
Safiya	sah-FEE-yah	Clear-minded, pure	Swahili E. Africa
Zakiya	zah-KEE-yah	Intelligent	Swahili, E. Africa

African Male Names

Name	Pronunciation	Meaning	Language and Country
Abasi	ah-BAH-see	Stern	Swahili, E. Africa
Ahmed	ah-HMED	Praiseworthy	Swahili, E. Africa
Babatunde	bah-bah-TOON-deh	Father returns	Yoruba, Nigeria
Dakarai	dah-KAH-rah-ee	Happiness	Shona, Zimbabwe
Gamba	GAM-bah	Warrior	Shona. Zimbabwe
Hasani	hah-SAH-nee	Handsome	Swahili, E. Africa

Jabari	jah-BAH-ree	Brave	Swahili, E. Africa
Kamau	Kah-MAH-oo	Quite warrior	Kikuyu, Kenya
Kofi	Koh-FEE	Born on Friday	Twi, Ghana
Oba	AW-bah	King	Yoruba, Nigeria
Olafemi	aw-lah-FEH-mee	Wealth, honor favors me	Yoruba, Nigeria
Omar	OH-mar	The highest (one of the Khalifah, followers of Muhammad)	Arabic, N. Africa
Useni	oo-SEH-nee	Tell me	Yao, Malawi
Yusuf	yoo-SOOF	He shall add (to his powers)	Swahili, E. Africa
Zuberi	zoo-BEH-ree	Strong	Swahili, E. Africa

AFROCENTRIC ESSAY

Now that you have completed the workbook, write an essay on what Afrocentricity means to you.

ADDENDUM I

Appropriate Answers to Afrocentric Self-Esteem Quiz

The following answers are appropriate because they reflect a high self-esteem that is desirable for African American youth.

Answer	Reason
1. No	There are over 400 million people of African descent in the world.
2. Yes	People of African descent built the world's first great civilizations in ancient Kemet (Egypt).
3. Yes	You are a very special person because everyone has a special quality given to him or her by the Creator.
4. Yes	You are a member of a strong and glorious race that has made great contributions to the world.
5. Yes	If you are serious and study hard, you can be an excellent student.
6. Yes	Your skin is beautiful because it is the color given to you by the Creator.
7. Yes	It is only natural and right for every individual to have racial pride.
8. Yes	Life is full of challenges and you must be prepared to face them to achieve your true potential.
9. Yes	Having pride in oneself is important because it helps you to have confidence and deal with difficult situations.
10. Yes	Alcohol and drugs are known to make people have low self-esteem and they are harmful to you.

Rating	Level of Self-Esteem
8 - 10	High Self-Esteem
5 - 7	Medium Self-Esteem
1 - 4	Low Self-Esteem

Note: If you rated low, do not be discouraged because you can develop a high self-esteem by applying some of the principles in this workbook to your life.

ADDENDUM II

REFERENCE BOOKS

The following books are recommended for acquiring additional information about the positive development of African American youth:

An Afrocentric Educational Manual: Toward a Non-Deficit Perspective in Services to Families and Children, Jualynee E. Dodson, Atlanta University School of Social Work.

A Model for Developing Programs for Black Children, Black Child Development Institute, Inc. 1463 Rhode Island Avenue, N.W., Washington, D.C. 20005.

A Non-Racist Framework for the Analysis of Educational Programs for Black Children, Margaret King. R&E Research Associates, Inc., 936 Industrial Avenue, Palo Alto, California 94303.

Educational Alternatives for Colonized People Models for Liberation, Robert L. Williams. Dunellen, New York.

A Guidebook for Planning Alcohol Presentation Programs with Black Youth, U.S. Department of Health & Human Services, Washington, D.C.

Working With Teen Parents: A Survey of Promising Approaches, Family Resource Coalition, Chicago, Illinois.

Challenges: A Young Man's Journal for Self-Awareness and Personal Planning, Advocacy Press, Santa Barbara, California.

Peer Education Programs, Center for Population Options, 2031 Florida Avenue, Washington, D.C.

A Resource Guide on Black Children and Youth, Institute for Urban Affairs & Research, Howard University, Washington, D.C.

Portrait of Inequality: Black and White Children in America, America's Children and Their Families: Key Facts, Children's Defense Fund, 1520 New Hampshire Avenue, N.W., Washington, D.C. 20036.

The Resource Guide, Ben Johnson, Washington, D.C.

Home Is A Dirty Street: The Social Oppression of Black Children, Useni Eugene Perkins. Third World Press, Chicago, Illinois.

Black Youth in Crisis, Ernest Cashmere. George Allen, Boston, Massachusetts.

Hustling and Other Hard Work Life Styles in the Ghetto, Betty Lou Valentine. The Free Press, New York, New York.

The Black Underclass: Poverty, Unemployment and Entrapment of Ghetto Youth, Douglas G. Glasgow. Vintage Books, New York.

Different Strokes: Pathways to Maturity in the Boston Ghetto, Ford Foundation Report. Westview Press, Boulder, Colorado.

Black Children: Their Roots, Culture and Learning Styles, Janice E. Hale. Brigham Young University Press.

Countering the Conspiracy to Destroy Black Boys, Jawanza Kunjufu. Afro-Am Publishing Co., Chicago, Illinois.

Image of A Man, Michael Brown. East Publications, Brooklyn, New York.

Developing Masculinity: The Black Male's Role in American Society, Robert Staples. Black Scholar Press.

Tomorrow's Tomorrow: The Black Woman, Joyce A. Ladner. Anchor Books, Garden City, New York.

The Developmental Psychology of the Black Child, Amos N. Wilson. Africana Research Publications, New York, New York.

Black Children Just Keep On Growing Alternative Curriculum Models for Young Black Children, Black Child Development Institute.

The Survival of Black Children & Youth, National Council for Black Child Development, Nuclassics and Science Publishing Co., Washington, D.C.

Children of Bondage: The Personality of Negro Youth In the Urban South, Allison Davis and John Dollard.

Negro Youth at the Crossways: Their Personality Development in the Middle States, E. Franklin Frazier.

Growing Up In The Black Belt: Negro Youth in the Rural South, Charles Johnson.

Dating Habits of Young Black Americans, John Porter. Kendall/Hunt Publishing Co., Dubuque, Iowa 52001.

Growing Up (Sex Education), Dr. James Docherty, Lika Publishing Foundation, Lagos, Nigeria.

Transformation: Rites of Passage Manual for African American Girls, Moore, Gilyard, King-McCreary, Warfield-Coppack, Stars Press, New York.

Readings on Black Children and Youth, Lula A. Beatty, Howard University.

A Rites of Passage Resource Manual, Nsenga Warfield-Coppack and Aminifu R. Harvey. Moat Institute for Human and Organizational Enhancement, Inc., Washington, D.C.

Afrocentricity: Theory of Social Change, Molefi Kete Asante. Amulefi Publishing, New York.

Bringing the Black Boy to Manhood: The Passage, Nathan Hare & Julia Hare. Black Think Tank, San Francisco, California.

Rites of Passage Program for Black Youth, E. Sims. B.E.R. Publications, Philadelphia.

Harvesting New Generations: The Positive Development of Black Youth, Useni Perkins. Third World Press.

Black Men: Obsolete, Single, Dangerous? Afrikan American Families in Transition, Essays in Discovery, Solution and Hope, Haki Madhubuti. Third World Press.

RISE BLACK YOUTH!

a new harvest
must be planted
to help future generations
blossom into adulthood
with values and knowledge
which liberate their minds
from the shackles of oppression
and the social diseases
that contaminate their lives

Rise Black youth!
take hold of your roots
Rise Black youth!
take control of your present

a new harvest
must be cultivated
so Black youth can fulfill
their true potential
and become the energizers
for preserving Black traditions
raising strong families
developing positive images
and building Black institutions

Rise Black youth!
take hold of your identity
Rise Black youth!
take control of your minds

a new harvest
must be sowed
that germinates
from our African vestiges
and embodies the wisdom
of our ancestors
to prepare Black youth
for their Rites of Passage
and ascension to adulthood

Rise Black youth!
take hold of your lives
Rise Black youth!
Take command of your destiny

UEP

Useni Eugene Perkins is a poet, playwright and social practitioner whose works have been widely published. He is also the editor of Black Child Journal. His social commentary on Black children, Home is a Dirty Street, was cited by Lerone Bennet, Jr. as ". . . one of the most important books on the sociology of the streets since publication of Black Metropolis." Mr. Perkins has been the recipient of a Chicago Community Trust Fellowship and is recognized as an authority on African American youth. His most recent works include Harvesting New Generations: The Positive Development of Black Youth and Explosion of Chicago's Black Street Gangs, both published by Third World Press. Among his many produced plays are Black Fairy, Image Makers, Professor J.B., Legend of Deadwood Dick, The Murder of Steve Biko and The Last Phoenix.

Children's Books Available From Third World Press

The Afrocentric Self Inventory and Discovery Workbook for African American Youth

A workbook designed to help African American youth understand and appreciate the African American value system and culture. This unique manual aids Black youth in discovering the rich legacy, heritage, and tradition of our people. $5.95

The Day They Stole The Letter J

An original and amusing story, full of surprises, with unique and perceptive illustrations. Join Jelani and Jerome as they journey through the exciting, frightening world of "The Letter J."$3.95

A Sound Investment

A collection of short stories for grades 5-8 which challenges young readers and builds integrity. Each story includes discussion questions to strengthen vocabulary and reading comprehension. *A Sound Investment* promotes the ideas of collective work , sharing, and justice. $2.95

The Tiger Who Wore White Gloves

Veteran writer and Poet Laureate of Illinois Gwendolyn Brooks and illustrator Timothy Jones have come together to produce a tool for young children which is educational as well as entertaining. This rhythmic and colorful story employs the animals of Africa, America, and Asia to teach children to accept and be proud of themselves. $6.95

The Story of Kwanzaa

A primary level reader offering a luminous and concise introduction to the tradition of Kwanzaa. An excellent way to teach children about this important African American holiday. $4.95

Order from **Order Department, Third World Press,** 7524 South Cottage Grove Avenue, Chicago, IL 60619. Shipping add $2.50 for first book and .50 shipping or each additional book. Mastercard/Visa orders may be placed by calling **(312) 651-0700.**